THE SEASIDE AND
THE FIRESIDE

THE SEASIDE AND THE FIRESIDE

BY
HENRY WADSWORTH LONGFELLOW

1850

WORDWELL
enterprises

CONTENTS

DEDICATION

As one who, walking in the twilight gloom,
    Hears round about him voices as it darkens,
And seeing not the forms from which they come,
    Pauses from time to time, and turns and hearkens ;

So walking here in twilight, O my friends!
    I hear your voices, softened by the distance,
And pause, and turn to listen, as each sends
    His words of friendship, comfort, and assistance.

If any thought of mine, or sung or told,
    Has ever given delight or consolation,
Ye have repaid me back a thousand fold,
    By every friendly sign and salutation.

Thanks for the sympathies that ye have shown !
    Thanks for each kindly word, each silent token,
That teaches me, when seeming most alone,
    Friends are around us, though no word be spoken.

Kind messages, that pass from land to land;
    Kind letters, that betray the heart's deep history,
In which we feel the pressure of a hand,—
    One touch of fire, —and all the rest is mystery!

The pleasant books, that silently among
    Our household treasures take familiar places,
And are to us as if a living tongue
    Spake from the printed leaves or pictured faces!

HENRY WADSWORTH LONGFELLOW

Perhaps on earth I never shall behold,
    With eye of sense, your outward form and semblance;
Therefore to me ye never will grow old,
    But live for ever young in my remembrance.

Never grow old, nor change, nor pass away!
    Your gentle voices will flow on for ever,
When life grows bare and tarnished with decay,
    As through a leafless landscape flows a river.

Not chance of birth or place has made us friends,
    Being oftentimes of different tongues and nations,
But the endeavour for the selfsame ends,
    With the same hopes, and fears, and aspirations.

Therefore I hope to join your seaside walk,
    Saddened, and mostly silent, with emotion;
Not interrupting with intrusive talk
    The grand, majestic symphonies of ocean.

BY THE SEASIDE

THE BUILDING OF THE SHIP

"Build me straight, O worthy Master!
    Stanch and strong, a goodly vessel,
That shall laugh at all disaster,
    And with wave and whirlwind wrestle!"

The merchant's word
Delighted the Master heard;
For his heart was in his work, and the heart
Giveth grace unto every Art.

A quiet smile played round his lips,
As the eddies and dimples of the tide
Play round the bows of ships,
That steadily at anchor ride.
And with a voice that was full of glee,
He answered, "Ere long we will launch
A vessel as goodly, and strong, and stanch,
As ever weathered a wintry sea!"

And first with nicest skill and art,
Perfect and finished in every part,
A little model the Master wrought,
Which should be to the larger plan
What the child is to the man,
Its counterpart in miniature;
That with a hand more swift and sure
The greater labor might be brought
To answer to his inward thought.
And as he labored, his mind ran o'er

The various ships that were built of yore,
And above them all, and strangest of all
Towered the Great Harry, crank and tall,
Whose picture was hanging on the wall,
With bows and stern raised high in air,
And balconies hanging here and there,
And signal lanterns and flags afloat,
And eight round towers, like those that frown
From some old castle, looking down
Upon the drawbridge and the moat.
And he said with a smile, "Our ship, I wis,
Shall be of another form than this!"

It was of another form, indeed;
Built for freight, and yet for speed,
A beautiful and gallant craft;
Broad in the beam, that the stress of the blast,
Pressing down upon sail and mast,
Might not the sharp bows overwhelm;
Broad in the beam, but sloping ast
With graceful curve and slow degrees,
That she might be docile to the helm,
And that the currents of parted seas,
Closing behind, with mighty force,
Might aid and not impede her course.

In the ship-yard stood the Master,
    With the model of the vessel,
That should laugh at all disaster,
    And with wave and whirlwind wrestle!

Covering many a rood of ground,
Lay the timber piled around ;
Timber of chestnut, and elm, and oak,
And scattered here and there, with these,
The knarred and crooked cedar knees;

Brought from regions far away,
From Pascagoula's sunny bay,
And the banks of the roaring Roanoke !
Ah! what a wondrous thing it is
To note how many wheels of toil
One thought, one word, can set in motion !
There's not a ship that sails the ocean,
But every climate, every soil,
Must bring its tribute, great or small,
And help to build the wooden wall!

The sun was rising o'er the sea,
And long the level shadows lay,
As if they, too, the beams would be
Of some great, airy argosy,
Framed and launched in a single day.
That silent architect, the sun,
Had hewn and laid them every one,
Ere the work of man was yet begun.
Beside the Master, when he spoke,
A youth, against an anchor leaning,
Listened, to catch his slightest meaning.
Only the long waves, as they broke
In ripples on the pebbly beach,
Interrupted the old man's speech.

Beautiful they were, in sooth,
The old man and the fiery youth !
The old man, in whose busy brain
Many a ship that sailed the main
Was modelled o'er and o'er again;—
The fiery youth, who was to be
The heir of his dexterity,
The heir of his house, and his daughter's hand,
When he had built and launched from land
What the elder head had planned.

13

"Thus," said he, " will we build this ship!
Lay square the blocks upon the slip,
And follow well this plan of mine.
Choose the timbers with greatest care;
Of all that is unsound beware;
For only what is sound and strong
To this vessel shall belong.
Cedar of Maine and Georgia pine
Here together shall combine.
A goodly frame, and a goodly fame,
And the Union be her name!
For the day that gives her to the sea
Shall give my daughter unto thee!

The Master's word
Enraptured the young man heard;
And as he turned his face aside,
With a look of joy and a thrill of pride,
Standing before
Her father's door,
He saw the form of his promised bride.
The sun shone on her golden hair,
And her cheek was glowing fresh and fair,
With the breath of morn and the soft sea air.
Like a beauteous barge was she,
Still at rest on the sandy beach,
Just beyond the billow's reach;
But he
Was the restless, seething, stormy sea!

Ah, how skilful grows the hand
That obeyeth Love's command !
It is the heart, and not the brain,
That to the highest doth attain,
And he who followeth Love's behest
Far exceedeth all the rest !

Thus with the rising of the sun
Was the noble task begun,
And soon throughout the ship-yard's bounds
Were heard the intermingled sounds
Of axes and of mallets, plied
With vigorous arms on every side;
Plied so deftly and so well,
That, ere the shadows of evening fell,
The keel of oak for a noble ship,
Scarfed and bolted, straight and strong,
Was lying ready, and stretched along
The blocks, well placed upon the slip.
Happy, thrice happy, every one
Who sees his labor well begun,
And not perplexed and multiplied,
By idly waiting for time and tide!

And when the hot, long day was o'er,
The young man at the Master's door
Sat with the maiden calm and still.
And within the porch, a little more
Removed beyond the evening chill,
The father sat, and told them tales
Of wrecks in the great September gales,
Of pirates upon the Spanish Main,
And ships that never came back again,
 The chance and change of a sailor's life,
 Want and plenty, rest and strife,
 His roving fancy, like the wind,
 That nothing can stay and nothing can bind,
 And the magic charm of foreign lands,
 With shadows of palms, and shining sands,
 Where the tumbling surf,
 O'er the coral reefs of Madagascar,
 Washes the feet of the swarthy Lascar,
 As he lies alone and asleep on the turf.

And the trembling maiden held her breath
At the tales of that awful, pitiless sea,
With all its terror and mystery,
The dim, dark sea, so like unto Death,
That divides and yet unites mankind!
And whenever the old man paused, a gleam
From the bowl of his pipe would awhile illume
The silent group in the twilight gloom,
And thoughtful faces, as in a dream;
And for a moment one might mark
What had been hidden by the dark,
That the head of the maiden lay at rest,
Tenderly, on the young man's breast!

Day by day the vessel grew,
With timbers fashioned strong and true,
Stemson and keelson and sternson-knee,
Till, framed with perfect symmetry,
A skeleton ship rose up to view!
And around the bows and along the side
The heavy hammers and mallets plied,
Till after many a week, at length,
Wonderful for form and strength,
Sublime in its enormous bulk,
Loomed aloft the shadowy hulk!

And around it columns of smoke, upwreathing,
Rose from the boiling, bubbling, seething
Caldron, that glowed,
And overflowed
With the black tar, heated for the sheathing.
And amid the clamors
Of clattering hammers,
He who listened heard now and then
The song
of the Master and his men:

"Build me straight, O worthy Master,
   Stanch and strong, a goodly vessel,
That shall laugh at all disaster,
   And with wave and whirlwind wrestle ! "

With oaken brace and copper band,
Lay the rudder on the sand,
That, like a thought, should have control
Over the movement of the whole;
And near it the anchor, whose giant hand
Would reach down and grapple with the land,
And immovable and fast
Hold the great ship against the bellowing blast!
And at the bows an image stood,
By a cunning artist carved in wood,
With robes of white, that far behind
Seemed to be fluttering in the wind.
It was not shaped in a classic mould,
Not like a Nymph or Goddess of old,
Or Naiad rising from the water,
But modelled from the Master's daughter!
On many a dreary and misty night,
'T will be seen by the rays of the signal light,
Speeding along through the rain and the dark,
Like a ghost in its snow-white sark,
The pilot of some phantom bark,
Guiding the vessel, in its flight,
By a path none other knows aright!

Behold, at last,
Each tall and tapering mast
Is swung into its place;
Shrouds and stays
Holding it firm and fast !

Long ago,
In the deer-haunted forests of Maine,
When upon mountain and plain
Lay the snow,
They fell, —those lordly pines!
Those grand, majestic pines!
'Mid shouts and cheers
The jaded steers,
Panting beneath the goad,
Dragged down the weary, winding road
Those captive kings so straight and tall,
To be shorn of their streaming hair,
And, naked and bare,
To feel the stress and the strain
Of the wind and the reeling main,
Whose roar
Would remind them for evermore
Of their native forests they should not see again.

And everywhere
The slender, graceful spars
Poise aloft in the air,
And at the mast head,
White, blue, and red,
A flag unrolls the stripes and stars.
Ah ! when the wanderer, lonely, friendless,
In foreign harbours shall behold
That flag unrolled,
'T will be as a friendly hand
Stretched out from his native land,
Filling his heart with memories sweet and endless!

All is finished! and at length
Has come the bridal day
Of beauty and of strength.
To-day the vessel shall be launched!

With fleecy clouds the sky is blanched,
And o'er the bay,
Slowly, in all his splendors dight,
The great sun rises to behold the sight.

The ocean old,
Centuries old,
 Strong as youth, and as uncontrolled,
Paces restless to and fro,
Up and down the sands of gold.
His beating heart is not at rest ;
And far and wide,
With ceaseless flow,
His beard of snow
Heaves with the heaving of his breast.

He waits impatient for his bride.
There she stands,
With her foot upon the sands,
Decked with flags and streamers gay,
In honor of her marriage day,
Her snow-white signals fluttering, blending,
Round her like a veil descending,
Ready to be
The bride of the gray, old sea.

On the deck another bride
Is standing by her lover's side.
Shadows from the flags and shrouds,
Like the shadows cast by clouds,
Broken by many a sunny fleck,
Fall around them on the deck.

The prayer is said
The service read,
The joyous bridegroom bows his head;

And in tears the good old Master
Shakes the brown hand of his son,
Kisses his daughter's glowing cheek
In silence, for he cannot speak,
And ever faster
Down his own the tears begin to run.
The worthy pastor—
The shepherd of that wandering flock,
That has the ocean for its wold,
That has the vessel for its fold,
Leaping ever from rock to rock—
Spake, with accents mild and clear,
Words of warning, words of cheer,
But tedious to the bridegroom's ear.
He knew the chart
Of the sailor's heart,
All its pleasures and its griefs,
All its shallows and rocky reefs,
All those secret currents, that flow
With such resistless undertow,
And lift and drift, with terrible force,
The will from its moorings and its course.
Therefore he spake, and thus said he:—

"Like unto ships far off at sea,
Outward or homeward bound, are we.
Before, behind, and all around,
Floats and swings the horizon's bound,
Seems at its outer rim to rise
And climb the crystal wall of the skies,
And then again to turn and sink,
As if we could slide from its outer brink.
Ah! it is not the sea,
It is not the sea that sinks and shelves,
But ourselves
That rock and rise

With endless and uneasy motion,
Now touching the very skies,
Now sinking into the depths of ocean.
Ah! if our souls but poise and swing
Like the compass in its brazen ring,
Ever level and ever true
To the toil and the task we have to do,
We shall sail securely, and safely reach
The Fortunate Isles, on whose shining beach
The sights we see, and the sounds we hear,
Will be those of joy and not of fear!"

Then the Master,
With a gesture of command,
Waved his hand;
And at the word,
Loud and sudden there was heard,
All around them and below,
The sound of hammers, blow on blow,
Knocking away the shores and spurs.
And see! she stirs!
She starts, —she moves, —she seems to feel
The thrill of life along her keel,
And, spurning with her foot the ground,
With one exulting, joyous bound,
She leaps into the ocean's arms!

And lo! from the assembled crowd
There rose a shout, prolonged and loud,
That to the ocean seemed to say,
"Take her, O bridegroom, old and gray,
Take her to thy protecting arms,
With all her youth and all her charms!"

How beautiful she is! How fair
She lies within those arms, that press

Her form with many a soft caress
Of tenderness and watchful care!

Sail forth into the sea, O ship!
Through wind and wave, right onward steer!
The moistened eye, the trembling lip,
Are not the signs of doubt or fear.

Sail forth into the sea of life,
O gentle, loving, trusting wife,
And safe from all adversity
Upon the bosom of that sea
Thy comings and thy goings be!
For gentleness and love and trust
Prevail o'er angry wave and gust;
And in the wreck of noble lives
Something immortal still survives!

Thou, too, sail on, O Ship of State!
Sail on, O UNION, strong and great!
Humanity with all its fears,
With all the hopes of future years,
Is hanging breathless on thy fate!

We know what Master laid thy keel,
What Workmen wrought thy ribs of steel,
Who made each mast, and sail, and rope,
What anvils rang, what hammers beat,
In what a forge and what a heat
Were shaped the anchors of thy hope!
Fear not each sudden sound and shock,
'T is of the wave and not the rock;
'Tis but the fapping of the sail,
And not a rent made by the gale!
In spite of rock and tempest roar,
In spite of false lights on the shore,

Sail on, nor fear to breast the sea !
Our hearts, our hopes, are all with thee,
Our hearts, our hopes, our prayers, our tears,
Our faith triumphant o'er our fears,
Are all with thee, -are all with thee!

THE EVENING STAR

Just above yon sandy bar,
    As the day grows fainter and dimmer,
Lonely and lovely, a single star
    Lights the air with a dusky glimmer.

Into the ocean faint and far
    Falls the trail of its golden splendor,
And the gleam of that single star
    Is ever refulgent, soft, and tender.

Chrysaor rising out of the sea,
    Showed thus glorious and thus emulous,
Leaving the arms of Callirrhoe,
    For ever tender, soft, and tremulous.

Thus o'er the ocean faint and far
    Trailed the gleam of his falchion brightly;
Is it a God, or is it a star
    That, entranced, I gaze on nightly!

THE SECRET OF THE SEA

Ah! what pleasant visions haunt me
    As I gaze upon the sea!
All the old romantic legends,
    All my dreams, come back to me.

Sails of silk and ropes of sendal,
    Such as gleam in ancient lore;
And the singing of the sailors,
    And the answer from the shore!

Most of all, the Spanish ballad
    Haunts me oft, and tarries long,
Of the noble Count Arnaldos
    And the sailor's mystic song.

Like the long waves on a sea-beach,
    Where the sand as silver shines,
With a soft, monotonous cadence,
    Flow its unrhymed lyric lines;—

Telling how the Count Arnaldos,
    With his hawk upon his hand,
Saw a fair and stately galley,
    Onward steering to the land;—

How he heard the ancient helmsman
    Chant a song so wild and clear,
That the sailing sea-bird slowly
    Poised upon the mast to hear,

Till his soul was full of longing,
  And he cried, with impulse strong,—
"Helmsman ! for the love of heaven,
  Teach me, too, that wondrous song!

"Wouldst thou," —so the helmsman answered,
  "Learn the secret of the sea
Only those who brave its dangers
  Comprehend its mystery!"

In each sail that skims the horizon,
  In each landward-blowing breeze,
I behold that stately galley,
  Hear those mournful melodies;

Till my soul is full of longing
  For the secret of the sea,
And the heart of the great ocean
  Sends a thrilling pulse through me.

TWILIGHT

The twilight is sad and cloudy,
  The wind blows wild and free,
And like the wings of sea-birds
  Flash the white caps of the sea.

But in the fisherman's cottage
  There shines a ruddier light,
And a little face at the window
  Peers out into the night.

Close, close it is pressed to the window,
  As if those childish eyes
Were looking into the darkness,
  To see some form arise.

And a woman's waving shadow
  Is passing to and fro,
Now rising to the ceiling,
  Now bowing and bending low.

What tale do the roaring ocean,
  And the night-wind, bleak and wild,
As they beat at the crazy casement,
  Tell to that little child ?

And why do the roaring ocean,
  And the night-wind, wild and bleak,
As they beat at the heart of the mother,
  Drive the color from her cheek?

SIR HUMPHREY GILBERT

SOUTHWARD with fleet of ice
  Sailed the corsair Death;
Wild and fast blew the blast,
  And the east-wind was his breath.

His lordly ships of ice
  Glistened in the sun;
On each side, like pennons wide,
  Flashing crystal streamlets run.

His sails of white sea-mist
  Dripped with silver rain;
But where he passed there were cast
  Leaden shadows o'er the main.

Eastward from Campobello
  Sir Humphrey Gilbert sailed;
Three days or more seaward he bore,
  Then, alas! the land-wind failed.

Alas! the land-wind failed,
  And ice-cold grew the night;
And never more, on sea or shore,
  Should Sir Humphrey see the light.

He sat upon the deck,
  The Book was in his hand;
"Do not fear! Heaven is as near,"
  He said, "by water as by land!"

In the first watch of the night,
   Without a signal's sound,
Out of the sea, mysteriously,
   The fleet of Death rose all around.

The moon and the evening star
   Were hanging in the shrouds;
Every mast, as it passed,
   Seemed to rake the passing clouds.

They grappled with their prize,
   At midnight black and cold!
As of a rock was the shock;
   Heavily the ground-swell rolled.

Southward through day and dark,
   They drift in close embrace,
With mist and rain, to the Spanish Main;
   Yet there seems no change of place.

Southward, for ever southward,
   They drift through dark and day;
And like a dream, in the Gulf-Stream
   Sinking, vanish all away.

THE LIGHTHOUSE

The rocky ledge runs far into the sea,
  And on its outer point, some miles away,
The Lighthouse lifts its massive masonry,
  A pillar of fire by night, of cloud by day.

Even at this distance I can see the tides,
  Upheaving, break unheard along its base,
A speechless wrath, that rises and subsides
  In the white lip and tremor of the face.

And as the evening darkens, lo ! how bright,
  Through the deep purple of the twilight air,
Beams forth the sudden radiance of its light
  With strange, unearthly splendor in its glare!

Not one alone; from each projecting cape;
  And perilous reef along the ocean's verge,
Starts into life a dim, gigantic shape,
  Holding its lantern o'er the restless surge.

Like the great giant Christopher it stands
  Upon the brink of the tempestuous wave,
Wading far out among the rocks and sands,
  The night-o'ertaken mariner to save.

And the great ships sail outward and return,
  Bending and bowing o'er the billowy swells,
And ever joyful, as they see it burn,
  They wave their silent welcomes and farewells.

They come forth from the darkness, and their sails
    Gleam for a moment only in the blaze,
And eager faces, as the light unveils,
    Gaze at the tower, and vanish while they gaze.

The mariner remembers when a child,
    On his first voyage, he saw it fade and sink;
And when, returning from adventures wild,
    He saw it rise again o'er ocean's brink.

Steadfast, serene, immovable, the same
    Year after year, through all the silent night
Burns on for evermore that quenchless flame,
    Shines on that inextinguishable light !

It sees the ocean to its bosom clasp
    The rocks and sea-sand with the kiss of peace;
It sees the wild winds lift it in their grasp,
    And hold it up, and shake it like a fleece.

The startled waves leap over it; the storm
    Smites it with all the scourges of the rain,
And steadily against its solid form
    Press the great shoulders of the hurricane.

The sea-bird wheeling round it, with the din
    Of wings and winds and solitary cries,
Blinded and maddened by the light within,
    Dashes himself against the glare, and dies.

A new Prometheus, chained upon the rock,
    Still grasping in his hand the fire of Jove,
It does not hear the cry, nor heed the shock,
    But hails the mariner with words of love.

"Sail on!" it says, "sail on, ye stately ships!
    And with your floating bridge the ocean span;
Be mine to guard this light from all eclipse,
    Be yours to bring man nearer unto man!"

THE FIRE IN DRIFT-WOOD

We sat within the farm-house old,
  Whose windows, looking o'er the bay,
Gave to the sea-breeze, damp and cold,
  An easy entrance, night and day.

Not far away we saw the port,—
  The strange, old-fashioned, silent town,—
The light-house, —the dismantled fort,—
  The wooden houses, quaint and brown.

We sat and talked until the night,
  Descending, filled the little room;
Our faces faded from the sight,
  Our voices only broke the gloom.

We spake of many a vanished scene,
  Of what we once had thought and said,
Of what had been, and might have been,
  And who was changed, and who was dead;

And all that fills the hearts of friends,
  When first they feel, with secret pain,
Their lives thenceforth have separate ends,
  And never can be one again;

The first slight swerving of the heart,
  That words are powerless to express,
And leave it still unsaid in part,
  Or say it in too great excess.

The very tones in which we spake
    Had something strange, I could but mark;
The leaves of memory seemed to make
    A mournful rustling in the dark.

Oft died the words upon our lips,
    As suddenly, from out the fire
Built of the wreck of stranded ships,
    The flames would leap and then expire.

And, as their splendor flashed and failed,
    We thought of wrecks upon the main,—
Of ships dismasted, that were hailed
    And sent no answer back again.

The windows, rattling in their frames,—
    The ocean, roaring up the beach,—
The gusty blast, —the bickering flames,—
    All mingled vaguely in our speech;

Until they made themselves a part
    Of fancies floating through the brain,
The long-lost ventures of the heart,
    That send no answers back again.

O flames that glowed ! O hearts that yearned!
    They were indeed too much akin,
The drift-wood fire without that burned,
    The thoughts that burned and glowed within.

BY THE FIRESIDE

RESIGNATION

There is no flock, however watched and tended,
    But one dead lamb is there!
There is no fireside, howsoe'er defended,
    But has one vacant chair!

The air is full of farewells to the dying,
    And mournings for the dead;
The heart of Rachel, for her children crying,
    Will not be comforted!

Let us be patient! These severe afflictions
    Not from the ground arise,
But oftentimes celestial benedictions
    Assume this dark disguise.

We see but dimly through the mists and vapors;
    Amid these earthly damps
What seem to us but sad, funereal tapers
    May be heaven's distant lamps.

There is no Death! What seems so is transition;
    This life of mortal breath
Is but a suburb of the life elysian,
    Whose portal we call Death.

She is not dead, —the child of our affection,—
    But gone unto that school
Where she no longer needs our poor protection,
    And Christ himself doth rule.

In that great cloister's stillness and seclusion,
    By guardian angels led,
Safe from teniptation, safe from sin's pollution,
    She lives, whom we call dead.

Day after day we think what she is doing
    In those bright realms of air;
Year after year, her tender steps pursuing,
    Behold her grown more fair.

Thus do we walk with her, and keep unbroken
    The bond which nature gives,
Thinking that our remembrance, though unspoken,
    May reach her where she lives.

Not as a child shall we again behold her;
    For when with raptures wild
In our embraces we again enfold her,
    She will not be a child;

But a fair maiden, in her Father's mansion,
    Clothed with celestial grace ;
And beautiful with all the soul's expansion
    Shall we behold her face.

And though at times impetuous with emotion
    And anguish long suppressed,
The swelling heart heaves moaning like the ocean,
    That cannot be at rest,

We will be patient, and assuage the feeling
    We may not wholly stay;
By silence sanctifying, not concealing,
    The grief that must have way.

THE BUILDERS

All are architects of Fate,
    Working in these walls of Time;
Some with massive deeds and great,
    Some with ornaments of rhyme.

Nothing useless is, or low;
    Each thing in its place is best;
And what seems but idle show
    Strengthens and supports the rest.

For the structure that we raise,
    Time is with materials filled;
Our to-days and yesterdays
    Are the blocks with which we build.

Truly shape and fashion these ;
    Leave no yawning gaps between;
Think not, because no man sees,
    Such things will remain unseen.

In the elder days of Art,
    Builders wrought with greatest care
Each minute and unseen part;
    For the Gods see everywhere.

Let us do our work as well,
    Both the unseen and the seen ;
Make the house, where Gods may dwell,
    Beautiful, entire, and clean.

Else our lives are incomplete,
    Standing in these walls of Time,
Broken stairways, where the feet
    Stumble as they seek to climb.

Build to-day, then, strong and sure,
    With a firm and ample base;
And ascending and secure
    Shall to-morrow find its place.

Thus alone can we attain
    To those turrets, where the eye
Sees the world as one vast plain,
    And one boundless reach of sky.

SAND OF THE DESERT IN AN HOUR-GLASS

A HANDFUL of red sand, from the hot clime
    Of Arab deserts brought,
Within this glass becomes the spy of Time,
    The minister of Thought.

How many weary centuries has it been
    About those deserts blown!
How many strange vicissitudes has seen,
    How many histories known!

Perhaps the camels of the Ishmaelite
    Trampled and passed it o'er,
When into Egypt from the patriarch's sight
    His favorite son they bore.

Perhaps the feet of Moses, burnt and bare,
    Crushed it beneath their tread;
Or Pharaoh's flashing wheels into the air
    Scattered it as they sped;

Or Mary, with the Christ of Nazareth
    Held close in her caress,
Whose pilgrimage of hope and love and faith
    Illumed the wilderness;

Or anchorites beneath Engaddi's palms
    Pacing the Red Sea beach,
And singing slow their old Armenian psalms
    In half-articulate speech;

Or caravans, that from Bassora's gate
   With westward steps depart ;
Or Mecca's pilgrims, confident of Fate,
   And resolute in heart !

These have passed over it, or may have passed!
   Now in this crystal tower
Imprisoned by some curious hand at last,
   It counts the passing hour.

And as I gaze, these narrow walls expand;—
   Before my dreamy eye
Stretches the desert with its shifting sand,
   Its unimpeded sky.

And borne aloft by the sustaining blast,
   This little golden thread
Dilates into a column high and vast,
   A form of fear and dread.

And onward, and across the setting sun,
   Across the boundless plain,
The column and its broader shadow run,
   Till thought pursues in vain.

The vision vanishes! These walls again
   Shut out the lurid sun,
Shut out the hot, immeasurable plain;
   The half-hour's sand is run!

BIRDS OF PASSAGE

Black shadows fall
From the lindens tall,
That lift aloft their massive wall
   Against the southern sky;

And from the realms
Of the shadowy elms
A tide-like darkness overwhelms
   The fields that round us lie.

But the night is fair,
And everywhere
A warm, soft, vapor fills the air,
   And distant sounds seem near ;

And above, in the light
Of the star-lit night,
Swift birds of passage wing their flight
   Through the dewy atmosphere.

I hear the beat
Of their pinions fleet,
As from the land of snow and sleet
   They seek a southern lea.

I hear the cry
Of their voices high
Falling dreamily through the sky,
   But their forms I cannot see.

O, say not so!
Those sounds that flow
In murmurs of delight and woe
　　Come not from wings of birds.

They are the throngs
Of the poet's songs,
Murmurs of pleasures, and pains, and wrongs,
　　The sound of winged words.

This is the cry
Of souls, that high
On toiling, beating pinions, fly,
　　Seeking a warmer clime.

From their distant flight
Through realms of light
It falls into our world of night,
　　With the murmuring sound of rhyme.

THE OPEN WINDOW

The old house by the lindens
   Stood silent in the shade,
And on the gravelled pathway
   The light and shadow played.

I saw the nursery windows
   Wide open to the air;
But the faces of the children,
   They were no longer there.

The large Newfoundland house-dog
   Was standing by the door;
He looked for his little playmates,
   Who would return no more.

They walked not under the lindens,
   They played not in the hall;
But shadow, and silence, and sadness
   Were hanging over all.

The birds sang in the branches,
   With sweet, familiar tone;
But the voices of the children
   Will be heard in dreams alone!

And the boy that walked beside me,
   He could not understand
Why closer in mine, ah! closer,
   I pressed his warm, soft hand!

KING WITLAF'S DRINKING-HORN

WITLAF, a king of the Saxons,
  Ere yet his last he breathed,
To the merry monks of Croyland
  His drinking-horn bequeathed,—

That, whenever they sat at their revels,
  And drank from the golden bowl,
They might remember the donor,
  And breathe a prayer for his soul.

So sat they once at Christmas,
  And bade the goblet pass;
In their beards the red wine glistened
  Like dew-drops in the grass.

They drank to the soul of Witlaf,
  They drank to Christ the Lord,
And to each of the Twelve Apostles,
  Who had preached his holy word.

They drank to the Saints and Martyrs
  Of the dismal days of yore,
And as soon as the horn was empty
  They remembered one Saint more.

And the reader droned from the pulpit,
  Like the murmur of many bees,
The legend of good Saint Guthlac,
  And Saint Basil's homilies;

Till the great bells of the convent,
 From their prison in the tower,
Guthlac and Bartholomæus,
 Proclaimed the midnight hour.

And the Yule-log cracked in the chimney,
 And the Abbot bowed his head,
And the flamelets flapped and flickered,
 But the Abbot was stark and dead.

Yet still in his pallid fingers
 He clutched the golden bowl,
In which, like a pearl dissolving,
 Had sunk and dissolved his soul.

But not for this their revels
 The jovial monks forbore,
For they cried, "Fill high the goblet!
 We must drink to one Saint more!"

GASPAR BECERRA

By his evening fire the artist
    Pondered o'er his secret shame;
Baffled, weary, and disheartened,
    Still he mused, and dreamed of fame.

'T was an image of the Virgin
    That had tasked his utmost skill ;
But alas! his fair ideal
    Vanished and escaped him still.

From a distant Eastern island
    Had the precious wood been brought;
Day and night the anxious master
    At his toil untiring wrought;

Till, discouraged and desponding,
    Sat he now in shadows deep,
And the day's humiliation
    Found oblivion in sleep.

Then a voice cried, "Rise, O master!
    From the burning brand of oak
Shape the thought that stirs within thee!"
    And the startled artist woke,—

Woke, and from the smoking embers
    Seized and quenched the glowing wood;
And therefrom he carved an image,
    And he saw that it was good.

HENRY WADSWORTH LONGFELLOW

O thou sculptor, painter, poet!
   Take this lesson to thy heart:
That is best which lieth nearest;
   Shape from that thy work of art.

PEGASUS IN POUND

Once into a quiet village,
    Without haste and without heed,
In the golden prime of morning,
    Strayed the poet's winged steed.

It was Autumn, and incessant
    Piped the quails from shocks and sheaves,
And, like living coals, the apples
    Burned among the withering leaves.

Loud the clamorous bell was ringing
    From its belfry gaunt and grim;
'Twas the daily call to labor,
    Not a triumph meant for him.

Not the less he saw the landscape,
    In its gleaming vapor veiled;
Not the less he breathed the odors
    That the dying leaves exhaled.

Thus, upon the village common,
    By the school-boys he was found;
And the wise men, in their wisdom,
    Put him straightway into pound.

Then the sombre village crier,
    Ringing loud his brazen bell,
Wandered down the street proclaiming
\   There was an estray to sell.

And the curious country people,
  Rich and poor, and young and old,
Came in haste to see this wondrous
  Winged steed, with mane of gold.

Thus the day passed, and the evening
  Fell, with vapors cold and dim;
But it brought no food nor shelter,
  Brought no straw nor stall, for him.

Patiently, and still expectant,
  Looked he through the wooden bars,
Saw the moon rise o'er the landscape,
  Saw the tranquil, patient stars ;

Till at length the bell at midnight
  Sounded from its dark abode,
And, from out a neighbouring farm-yard,
  Loud the cock Alectryon crowed.

Then, with nostrils wide distended,
  Breaking from his iron chain,
And unfolding far his pinions,
  To those stars he soared again.

On the morrow, when the village
  Woke to all its toil and care,
Lo! the strange steed had departed,
  And they knew not when nor where.

But they found, upon the greensward
  Where his struggling hoofs had trod,
Pure and bright, a fountain flowing
  From the hoof-marks in the sod.

From that hour, the fount unfailing
    Gladdens the whole region round,
Strengthening all who drink its waters,
    While it soothes them with its sound.

TEGNÉR'S DEATH

I heard a voice that cried,
"Balder the Beautiful
Is dead, is dead!"
And through the misty air
Passed like a mournful cry
Of sunward sailing cranes.

I saw the pallid corpse
Of the dead sun
Borne through the Northern sky.
Blasts from Niffelheim
Lifted the sheeted mists
Around him as he passed.

And the voice for ever cried,
"Balder the Beautiful
Is dead, is dead!"
And died away
Through the dreary night,
In accents of despair.

Balder the Beautiful,
God of the summer sun,
Fairest of all the Gods!
Light from his forehead beamed,
Runes were upon his tongue,
As on the warrior's sword.

All things in earth and air
Bound were by magic spell
Never to do him harm;
Even the plants and stones;
All save the mistletoe,
The sacred mistletoe!

Hæder, the blind old God,
Whose feet are shod with silence,
Pierced through that gentle breast
With his sharp spear, by fraud
Made of the mistletoe,
The accursed mistletoe!

They laid him in his ship,
With horse and harness,
As on a funeral pyre.
Odin placed
A ring upon his finger,
And whispered in his ear.

They launched the burning ship!
It Aoated far away
Over the misty sea,
Till like the moon it seemed,
Sinking beneath the waves.
Balder returned no more!

So perish the old Gods!
But out of the sea of Time
Rises a new land of song,
Fairer than the old.
Over its meadows green
Walk the young bards and sing.

Build it again,
O ye bards,
Fairer than before!
Ye fathers of the new race,
Feed upon morning dew,
Sing the new Song of Love!

The law of force is dead!
The law of love prevails!
Thor, the thunderer,
Shall rule the earth no more,
No more, with threats,
Challenge the meek Christ.

Sing no more,
O ye bards of the North,
Of Vikings and of Jarls!
Of the days of Eld
Preserve the freedom only,
Not the deeds of blood!

SONNET

On Mrs. Kemble's Readings from Shakspweare.

O Precious evenings! all too swiftly sped!
Leaving us heirs to amplest heritages
Of all the best thoughts of the greatest sages,
And giving tongues unto the silent dead!
How our hearts glowed and trembled as she read,
Interpreting by tones the wondrous pages
Of the great poet who foreruns the ages,
Anticipating all that shall be said!

O happy Reader! having for thy text
The magic book, whose Sibylline leaves have caught
The rarest essence of all human thought!
O happy Poet ! by no critic vext!
How must thy listening spirit now rejoice
To be interpreted by such a voice!

THE SINGERS

INSCRIPTION FOR AN ANTIQUE PITCHER

God sent his Singers upon earth
With songs of sadness and of mirth,
That they might touch the hearts of men,
And bring them back to heaven again.

The first, a youth, with soul of fire,
Held in his hand a golden lyre ;
Through groves he wandered, and by streams,
Playing the music of our dreams.

The second, with a bearded face,
Stood singing in the market-place,
And stirred with accents deep and loud
The hearts of all the listening crowd.

A gray, old man, the third and last,
Sang in cathedrals dim and vast,
While the majestic organ rolled
Contrition from its mouths of gold.

And those who heard the Singers three
Disputed which the best might be;
For still their music seemed to start
Discordant echoes in each heart.

But the great Master said, "I see
No best in kind, but in degree;
I gave a various gift to each,
To charm, to strengthen, and to teach.

"These are the three great chords of might,
And he whose ear is tuned aright
Will hear no discord in the three,
But the most perfect harmony."

SUSPIRIA

Take them, O Death! and bear away
Whatever thou canst call thine own!
Thine image, stamped upon this clay,
Doth give thee that, but that alone!

Take them, O Grave! and let them lie
Folded upon thy narrow shelves,
As garments by the soul laid by,
And precious only to ourselves!

Take them, O great Eternity!
Our little life is but a gust,
That bends the branches of thy tree,
And trails its blossoms in the dust!

HYMN

For my Brother's Ordination.

Christ to the young man said: "Yet one thing more;
    If thou wouldst perfect be,
Sell all thou hast and give it to the poor,
    And come and follow me!"

Within this temple Christ again, unseen,
    Those sacred words hath said,
And his invisible hands to-day have been
    Laid on a young man's head.

And evermore beside him on his way
    The unseen Christ shall move,
That he may lean upon his arm and say,—
    "Dost thou, dear Lord, approve?"

Beside him at the marriage feast shall be,
    To make the scene more fair;
Beside him in the dark Gethsemane
    Of pain and midnight prayer.

O holy trust! O endless sense of rest!
    Like the beloved John
To lay his head upon the Saviour's breast,
    And thus to journey on!

THE BLIND GIRL OF CASTÈL-CUILLÈ

FROM THE GASCON OF JASMIN

Only the Lowland tongue of Scotland might
Rehearse this little tragedy aright;
Let me attempt it with an English quill ;
And take, O Reader, for the deed the will.

I.

At the foot of the mountain height
  Where is perched Castèl-Cuillè,
When the apple, the plum, and the almond tree
  In the plain below were growing white,
  This is the song one might perceive
On a Wednesday morn of Saint Joseph's Eve :
"The roads should blossom, the roads should bloom,
So fair a bride shall leave her home!
Should blossom and bloom with garlands gay,
So fair a bride shall pass to-day!"

This old Te Deum, rustic rites attending,
  Seemed from the clouds descending;
  When lo! a merry company
Of rosy village girls, clean as the eye,
  Each one with her attendant swain,
Came to the cliff, all singing the same strain;
Resembling there, so near unto the sky,
Rejoicing angels, that kind Heaven had sent
For their delight and our encouragement.

Together blending,
And soon descending
The narrow sweep
Of the hill-side steep,
They wind aslant
Towards Saint Amant,
Through leafy alleys
Of verdurous valleys
With merry sallies
Singing their chant:

"The roads should blossom, the roads should bloom,
So fair a bride shall leave her home!
Should blossom and bloom with garlands gay,
So fair a bride shall pass to-day!"

It is Baptiste, and his affianced maiden,
With garlands for the bridal laden!

The sky was blue; without one cloud of gloom,
    The sun of March was shining brightly,
And to the air the freshening wind gave lightly
    Its breathings of perfume.

When one beholds the dusky hedges blossom,
A rustic bridal, ah ! how sweet it is !
    To sounds of joyous melodies,
That touch with tenderness the trembling bosom,
        A band of maidens
        Gayly frolicking,
        A band of youngsters
        Wildly rollicking!
          Kissing,
          Caressing,

With fingers pressing,
  Till in the veriest
Madness of mirth, as they dance,
They retreat and advance,
  Trying whose laugh shall be loudest and merriest;
While the bride, with roguish eyes,
 Sporting with them, now escapes and cries:
  "Those who catch me
    Married verily
    This year shall be!"

And all pursue with eager haste,
And all attain what they pursue,
And touch her pretty apron fresh and new,
  And the linen kirtle round her waist.

Meanwhile, whence comes it that among
These youthful maidens fresh and fair,
So joyous, with such laughing air,
Baptiste stands sighing, with silent tongue?
  And yet the bride is fair and young!
Is it Saint Joseph would say to us all,
That love, o'er-hasty, precedeth a fall?
  O, no! for a maiden frail, I trow,
  Never bore so lofty a brow!
What lovers! they give not a single caress!
To see them so careless and cold to-day,
  These are grand people, one would say.
  What ails Baptiste? what grief doth him oppress?

It is, that, half way up the hill,
In yon cottage, by whose walls
Stand the cart-house and the stalls,
Dwelleth the blind orphan still,
Daughter of a veteran old ;
And you must know, one year ago,

That Margaret, the young and tender,
Was the village pride and splendor,
And Baptiste her lover bold.
Love, the deceiver, them ensnared;
For them the altar was prepared;
But alas! the summer's blight,
The dread disease that none can stay,
The pestilence that walks by night,
Took the young bride's sight away.
All at the father's stern command was changed;
Their peace was gone, but not their love estranged.
Wearied at home, ere long the lover fled;
Returned but three short days ago,
The golden chain they round him throw,
He is enticed, and onward led
To marry Angela, and yet
Is thinking ever of Margaret.

Then suddenly a maiden cried,
"Anna, Theresa, Mary, Kate!
Here comes the cripple Jane!" And by a fountain's side
A woman, bent and gray with years,
Under the mulberry-trees appears,
And all towards her run, as feet
As had they wings upon their feet.

It is that Jane, the cripple Jane,
Is a soothsayer, wary and kind.
She telleth fortunes, and none complain.
She promises one a village swain,
Another a happy wedding-day,
And the bride a lovely boy straightway.
All comes to pass as she avers;
She never deceives, she never errs.

But for this once the village seer
Wears a countenance severe,
And from beneath her eyebrows thin and white
Her two eyes flash like cannons bright
Aimed at the bridegroom in waistcoat blue,
Who, like a statue, stands in view;
Changing color, as well he might,
When the beldame wrinkled and gray
Takes the young bride by the hand,
And, with the tip of her reedy wand
Making the sign of the cross, doth say:—
"Thoughtless Angela, beware!
Lest, when thou weddest this false bridegroom,
Thou diggest for thyself a tomb!"
And she was silent; and the maidens fair
Saw from each eye escape a swollen tear;
But on a little streamlet silver-clear,
What are two drops of turbid rain?
Saddened a moment, the bridal train
Resumed the dance and song again;
The bridegroom only was pale with fear;—
And down green alleys
Of verdurous valleys,
With merry sallies,
They sang the refrain:—

"The roads should blossom, the roads should bloom,
So fair a bride shall leave her home!
Should blossom and bloom with garlands gay,
So fair a bride shall pass to-day! "

II.

And by suffering worn and weary,
But beautiful as some fair angel yet,
   Thus lamented Margaret,
   In her cottage lone and dreary:—

"He has arrived! arrived at last!
Yet Jane has named him not these three days past;
   Arrived! yet keeps aloof so far!
And knows that of my night he is the star

Knows that long months I wait alone, benighted,
And count the moments since he went away!
Come! keep the promise of that happier day,
That I may keep the faith to thee I plighted!
What joy have I without thee ? what delight?
Grief wastes my life, and makes it misery;
Day for the others ever, but for me
   For ever night! for ever night !
When he is gone 't is dark! my soul is sad!
I suffer! O my God! come, make me glad.
When he is near, no thoughts of day intrude;
Day has blue heavens, but Baptiste has blue eyes!
Within them shines for me a heaven of love,
A heaven all happiness, like that above,
   No more of grief! no more of lassitude!
Earth I forget, —and heaven, and all distresses,
When seated by my side my hand he presses;
   But when alone, remember all!
Where is Baptiste? he hears not when I call!

A branch of ivy, dying on the ground,
    I need some bough to twine around!
In pity come! be to my suffering kind!
True love, they say, in grief doth more abound!
    What then —when one is blind ?

"Who knows? perhaps I am forsaken!
Ah! woe is me! then bear me to my grave!
    O God! what thoughts within me waken!
Away! he will return! I do but rave!
    He will return ! I need not fear!
    He swore it by our Saviour dear;
    He could not come at his own will;
    Is weary, or perhaps is ill!
    Perhaps his heart, in this disguise,
    Prepares for me some sweet surprise!
But some one comes! Though blind, my heart can see!
And that deceives me not ! 't is he! 't is he!"
    And the door ajar is set,
    And poor, confiding Margaret
Rises, with outstretched arms, but sightless eyes;
'T is only Paul, her brother, who thus cries:—

"Angela the bride has passed!
    I saw the wedding guests go by;
Tell me, my sister, why were we not asked?
    For all are there but you and I!"

"Angela married! and not send
    To tell her secret unto me!
O, speak! who may the bridegroom be?"
"My sister, 't is Baptiste, thy friend!"

A cry the blind girl gave, but nothing said;
A milky whiteness spreads upon her cheeks;

77

An icy hand, as heavy as lead,
Descending, as her brother speaks,
Upon her heart, that has ceased to beat,
Suspends awhile its life and heat.
She stands beside the boy, now sore distressed,
A wax Madonna as a peasant dressed.

At length, the bridal song again
Brings her back to her sorrow and pain.

"Hark! the joyous airs are ringing!
Sister, dost thou hear them singing?
How merrily they laugh and jest!
Would we were bidden with the rest!
I would don my hose of homespun gray,
And my doublet of linen striped and gay;
Perhaps they will come ; for they do not wed
Till to-morrow at seven o'clock, it is said!"
"I know it!" answered Margaret;
Whom the vision, with aspect black as jet,
Mastered again ; and its hand of ice
Held her heart crushed, as in a vice!
"Paul, be not sad ! 'Tis a holiday ;
To-morrow put on thy doublet gay !
But leave me now for a while alone."
Away, with a hop and a jump, went Paul,
And, as he whistled along the hall,
Entered Jane, the crippled crone.

"Holy Virgin! what dreadful heat!
I am faint, and weary, and out of breath!
But thou art cold, —art chill as death;
My little friend! what ails thee, sweet?"
"Nothing! I heard them singing home the bride;
And, as I listened to the song,
I thought my turn would come ere long,

Thou knowest it is at Whitsuntide.
Thy cards forsooth can never lie,
To me such joy they prophesy,
Thy skill shall be vaunted far and wide
When they behold him at my side.
And poor Baptiste, what sayest thou?
It must seem long to him; —methinks I see him now!"
    Jane, shuddering, her hand doth press :
"Thy love I cannot all approve;
We must not trust too much to happiness;—
Go, pray to God, that thou mayst love him less!"
    "The more I pray, the more I love!
It is no sin, for God is on my side!"
It was enough ; and Jane no more replied.

Now to all hope her heart is barred and cold ;
    But to deceive the beldame old
    She takes a sweet, contented air;
    Speak of foul weather or of fair,
    At every word the maiden smiles!
    Thus the beguiler she beguiles;
So that, departing at the evening's close,
    She says, "She may be saved! she nothing knows!"

    Poor Jane, the cunning sorceress!
Now that thou wouldst, thou art no prophetess!
This morning, in the fulness of thy heart,
    Thou wast so, far beyond thine art !

III.

Now rings the bell, nine times reverberating,
And the white daybreak, stealing up the sky,
Sees in two cottages two maidens waiting,
    How differently!

Queen of a day, by flatterers caressed,
    The one puts on her cross and crown,
    Decks with a huge bouquet her breast,
    And flaunting, fluttering up and down,
    Looks at herself, and cannot rest.

    The other, blind, within her little room,
    Has neither crown nor flower's perfume;
But in their stead for something gropes apart,
    That in a drawer's recess doth lie,
And, 'neath her bodice of bright scarlet dye,
    Convulsive clasps it to her heart.

    The one, fantastic, light as air,
      'Mid kisses ringing,
      And joyous singing,
Forgets to say her morning prayer!

The other, with cold drops upon her brow,
    Joins her two hands, and kneels upon the floor,
And whispers, as her brother opes the door,
    "O God! forgive me now!"

    And then the orphan, young and blind,
    Conducted by her brother's hand,
    Towards the church, through paths unscanned,
    With tranquil air, her way doth wind.

Odors of laurel, making her faint and pale,
    Round her at times exhale,
And in the sky as yet no sunny ray,
    But brumal vapors gray.

    Near that castle, fair to see,
Crowded with sculptures old, in every part,
    Marvels of nature and of art,
      And proud of its name of high degree,
    A little chapel, almost bare
    At the base of the rock, is builded there;
    All glorious that it lifts aloof,
    Above each jealous cottage roof,
Its sacred summit, swept by autumn gales,
    And its blackened steeple high in air,
    Round which the osprey screams and sails.

    "Paul, lay thy noisy rattle by!"
Thus Margaret said. 66 Where are we? we ascend!"
    "Yes; seest thou not our journey's end?
Hearest not the osprey from the belfry cry?
The hideous bird, that brings ill luck, we know!
Dost thou remember when our father said,
    The night we watched beside his bed,
    'O daughter, I am weak and low;
Take care of Paul; I feel that I am dying!'
And thou, and he, and I, all fell to crying?
Then on the roof the osprey screamed aloud;
And here they brought our father in his shroud.
There is his grave; there stands the cross we set;
Why dost thou clasp me so, dear Margaret?
    Come in! The bride will be here soon:
Thou tremblest! O my God! thou art going to swoon!"

She could no more, —the blind girl, weak and weary!
Avoice seemed crying from that grave so dreary,
"What wouldst thou do, my daughter ?" —and she started;
    And quick recoiled, aghast, faint-hearted;
But Paul, impatient, urges ever more
    Her steps towards the open door;
And when, beneath her feet, the unhappy maid
Crushes the laurel near the house immortal,
And with her head, as Paul talks on again,
    Touches the crown of filigrane
    Suspended from the low-arched portal,
    No more restrained, no more afraid,
    She walks, as for a feast arrayed,
And in the ancient chapel's sombre night
    They both are lost to sight.

    At length the bell,
    With booming sound,
    Sends forth, resounding round,
Its hymeneal peal o'er rock and down the dell.
    It is broad day, with sunshine and with rain ;
    And yet the guests delay not long,
    For soon arrives the bridal train,
    And with it brings the village throng.

In sooth, deceit maketh no mortal gay,
For lo ! Baptiste on this triumphant day,
Mute as an idiot, sad as yester-morning,
Thinks only of the beldame's words of warning.

And Angela thinks of her cross, I wis;
To be a bride is all! The pretty lisper
Feels her heart swell to hear all round her whisper,
"How beautiful! how beautiful she is!"

But she must calm that giddy head,
For already the Mass is said;
  At the holy table stands the priest;
The wedding ring is blessed; Baptiste receives it;
Ere on the finger of the bride he leaves it,
  He must pronounce one word at least!
'Tis spoken; and sudden at the groomsman's side
"'T is he !" well-known voice has cried.
And while the wedding guests all hold their breath,
Opes the confessional, and the blind girl, see!
"Baptiste," she said, "since thou hast wished my death,
As holy water be my blood for thee!"
And calmly in the air a knife suspended!
Doubtless her guardian angel near attended,
  For anguish did its work so well,
  That, ere the fatal stroke descended,
    Lifeless she fell!

  At eve, instead of bridal verse,
  The De Profundis filled the air ;
  Decked with flowers a simple hearse
  To the church-yard forth they bear ;
  Village girls in robes of snow
  Follow, weeping as they go ;
  Nowhere was a smile that day,
No, ah no! for each one seemed to say:—

"The roads should mourn and be veiled in gloom,
So fair a corpse shall leave its home!
Should mourn and should weep, ah, well-away!
So fair a corpse shall pass to-day!"

A CHRISTMAS CAROL

FROM THE NOEI BOURGUIGNON DE GUY BARÔZAI.

I hear along our street
Pass the minstrel throngs;
Hark! They play so sweet,
On their hautboys, Christmas songs!
    Let us by the fire
    Ever higher
Sing them till the night expire!

In December ring
Every day the chimes;
Loud the gleemen sing
In the streets they're merry rhymes.
    Let us by the fire
    Ever higher
Sing them till the night expire.

Shepherds at the grange,
Where the Babe was born,
Sang, with many a change,
Christmas carols until morn.
    Let us by the fire
    Ever higher
Sing them till the night expire!

These good people sang
Songs devout and sweet;
While the rafters rang,
There they stood with freezing feet.

Let us by the fire
Ever higher
Sing them till the night expire.

Nuns in frigid cells
At this holy tide,
For want of something else,
Christmas songs at times have tried.
Let us by the fire
Ever higher
Sing them till the night expire!

Washerwomen old,
To the sound they beat,
Sing by rivers cold,
With uncovered heads and feet.
Let us by the fire
Ever higher
Sing them till the night expire!

Who by the fires stands
Stamps his feet and sings;
But he who blows his hands
Not so gay a carol brings.
Let us by the fire
Ever higher
Sing them till the night expire!

NOTES

The Building of the Ship (p. 11)

"Behold, at last,
Each tall and tapering mast
Is swung into its place."

I wish to anticipate a criticism on this passage by stating, that sometimes, though not usually, vessels are launched fully rigged and sparred. I have availed myself of the exception, as better suited to my purposes than the general rule; but the reader will see that it is neither a blunder nor a poetic license. On this subject a friend in Portland, Maine, writes me thus:—

"In this State, and also, I am told, in New York, ships are sometimes rigged upon the stocks, in order to save time, or to make a show. There was a fine, large ship launched last summer at Ellsworth, fully rigged and sparred. Some years ago a ship was launched here, with her rigging, spars, sails, and cargo aboard. She sailed the next day and —was never heard of again! I hope this will not be the fate of your poem!"

Sir Humphrey Gilbert (p. 31)

"When the wind abated and the vessels were near enough, the Admiral was seen constantly sitting in the stern, with a book in his hand. On the 9th of September he was seen for the last time, and was heard by the people of the Hind to say, 'We are as near heaven by sea as by land.' In the following night, the lights of the ship suddenly disappeared. The people in the other vessel kept a good lookout for him during the remainder of the voyage. On the 22d of September they arrived, through much tempest and peril, at Falmouth. But nothing more was seen or heard of the Admiral." — BELKNAP's *American Biography*, I. 203.

The Blind Girl of Castèl-Cuillè (p. 71)

The Blind Girl of Castèl-Cuillè. Jasmin, the author of this beautiful poem, is to the South of France what Burns is to the South of Scotland, —the representative of the heart of the people,— one of those happy bards who are born with their mouths full of birds (*la bouco pleno d'aouzelous*). He has written his own biography in a poetic form, and the simple narrative of his poverty, his struggles, and his triumphs, is very touching. He still lives at Agen, on the Garonne; and long may he live there to delight his native land with native songs!

The following description of his person and way of life is taken from the graphic pages of "Béarn and the Pyrenees," by Louisa Stuart Costello, whose charming pen has done so much to illustrate the French provinces and their literature.

"At the entrance of the promenade, Du Gravier, is a row of small houses, —some *cafés*, others shops, the indication of which is a painted cloth placed across the way, with the owner's name in bright gold letters, in the manner of the arcades in the streets, and their announcements. One of the most glaring of these was, we observed, a bright blue flag, bordered with gold ; on which, in large gold letters, appeared the name of "Jasmin, Coiffeur.' We entered, and were welcomed by a smiling, dark-eyed woman, who informed us that her husband was busy at that moment dressing a customer's hair, but he was desirous to receive us, and begged we would walk into his parlour at the back of the shop.

*   *   *   *   *

"She exhibited to us a laurel crown of gold, of delicate workmanship, sent from the city of Clemence Isaure, Toulouse, to the poet; who will probably one day take his place in the *capitoul*. Next came a golden cup, with an inscription in his honor, given by the citizens of Auch; a gold watch, chain, and seals, sent by the king, Louis Philippe; an emerald ring worn and presented by the lamented Duke of Orleans; a pearl pin, by the graceful Duchess, who, on the poet's visit to Paris accompanied by his son, received him in the words he puts into the mouth of Henri Quatre:—

> *Brabes Gascous!*
> *A moun amou per bous aou dibes creyre:*
> *Benès! benès! ey plazé de bous beyre:*
> *A proucha bous!'*

A fine service of linen, the offering of the town of Pau, after its citizens had given fêtes in his honor, and loaded him with caresses and praises; and nicknacks and jewels of all descriptions offered to him by lady-ambassadresses, and great lords; English.misses' and 'miladis'; and French, and foreigners of all nations who did or did not understand Gascon.

"All this, though startling, was not convincing; Jasmin, the barber, might only be a fashion, a *furore*, a caprice, after all, and it was evident that he knew how to get up a scene well. When we had become nearly tired of looking over these tributes to his genius, the door opened, and the poet himself appeared. His manner was free and unembarrassed, well-bred, and lively; he received our compliments naturally, and like one accustomed to homage; said he was ill, and unfortunately too hoarse to read any thing to us, or should have been delighted to do so. He spoke with a broad Gascon accent, and very rapidly and eloquently; ran over the story of his successes; told us that his grandfather had been a beggar, and all his family very poor;

89

that he was now as rich as he wished to be; his son placed in a good position at Nantes; then showed us his son's picture, and spoke of his disposition, to which his brisk little wife added, that, though no fool, he had not his father's genius, to which truth Jasmin assented as a matter of course. I told him of having seen mention made of him in an English review; which he said had been sent him by Lord Durham, who had paid him a visit; and I then spoke of 'Mi cal mouri' as known to me. This was enough to make him forget his hoarseness and every other evil : it would never do for me to imagine that that little song was his best composition; it was merely his first; he must try to read to me a little of 'L'Abuglo,' —a few verses of 'Françouneto'; —'You will be charmed,' said he; 'but if I were well, and you would give me the pleasure of your company for some time, if you were not merely running through Agen, I would kill you with weeping, —I would make you die with distress for my poor Margarido, —my pretty Françouneto!'

"He caught up two copies of his book, from a pile lying on the table, and making us sit close to him, he pointed out the French translation on one side, which he told us to follow while he read in Gascon. He began in a rich, soft voice, and as he advanced, the surprise of Hamlet on hearing the player-king recite the disasters of Hecuba was but a type of ours, to find ourselves carried away by the spell of his enthusiasm. His eyes swam in tears; he became pale and red; he trembled; he recovered himself; his face was now joyous, now exulting, gay, jocose; in fact, he was twenty actors in one; he rang the changes from Rachel to Bouffé; and he finished by delighting us, besides beguiling us of our tears, and overwhelming us with astonishment.

"He would have been a treasure on the stage; for he is still, though his first youth is past, remarkably goodlooking and striking ; with black, sparkling eyes, of intense expression; a fine, ruddy complexion ; a countenance of wondrous mobility; a good figure; and action full of fire and grace; he has handsome hands, which he uses with infinite effect; and, on the whole, he is the best actor of the kind I ever saw. I could now quite understand what a troubadour or *jongleur* might be, and I look upon Jasmin as a revived specimen of that extinct race. Such as he is might have been Gaucelm Faidit, of Avignon, the friend of Cœur de Lion, who lamented the death of the hero in such moving strains; such might have been Bernard de Ventadour, who sang the praises of Queen Elinore's beauty; such Geoffrey Rudel, of Blaye, on his own Garonne; such the wild Vidal: certain it is, that none of these troubadours of old could more move, by their singing or reciting, than Jasmin, in whom all their long-smothered fire and traditional magic seems reillumined.

"We found we had stayed hours instead of minutes with the poet; but he would not hear of any apology, only regretted that his voice was so out of tune, in consequence of a violent cold, under which he was really laboring, and hoped to see us again. He told us our countrywomen of Pau had laden him with kindness and attention, and spoke with such enthusiasm of the beauty of certain misses,' that I feared his little wife would feel somewhat piqued; but, on the contrary, she stood by, smiling and happy, and enjoying the stories of his triumphs. I remarked that he had restored the poetry of the troubadours; asked him if he knew their songs; and said he was worthy to stand at their head. I am, indeed, a troubadour,' said he, with energy; but I am far beyond them all; they were but beginners; they never composed a poem like my Françouneto! there are no poets in France now, —there cannot be; the language does not admit of it; where is the fire, the spirit, the expression, the tenderness, the force of the Gascon? French is but the ladder to reach to the first floor of Gascon, —how can you get up to a height except by a ladder!'

*   *   *   *   *

"I returned by Agen, after an absence in the Pyrenees of some months, and renewed my acquaintance with Jasmin and his dark-eyed wife. I did not expect that I should be recognized; but the moment I entered the little shop I was hailed as an old friend. 'Ah!' cried Jasmin, 'enfin la voilà encore!' I could not but be flattered by this recollection, but soon found it was less on my own account that I was thus welcomed, than because a circumstance had occurred to the poet which he thought I could perhaps explain. He produced several French newspapers, in which he pointed out to me an article headed

'Jasmin à Londres'; being a translation of certain notices of himself, which had appeared in a leading English literary journal. He had, he said, been informed of the honor done him by numerous friends, and assured me his fame had been much spread by this means; and he was so delighted on the occasion, that he had resolved to learn English, in order that he might judge of the translations from his works, which, he had been told, were well done. I enjoyed his 'surprise, while I informed him that I knew who was the reviewer and translator; and explained the reason for the verses giving pleasure in an English dress to be the superior simplicity of the English language over modern French, for which he has a great contempt, as unfitted for lyrical composition. He inquired of me respecting Burns, to whom he had been likened ; and begged me to tell him something of Moore. The delight of himself and his wife was amusing, at having discovered a secret which had puzzled them so long.

"He had a thousand things to tell me ; in particular, that he had only the day before received a letter from the Duchess of Orleans, informing him that she had ordered a medal of her late husband to be struck, the first of which would be sent to him: she also announced to him the agreeable news of the king having granted him a pension of a thousand francs. He smiled and wept by turns, as he told all this; and declared, much as he was elated at the possession of a sum which made him a rich man for life, the kindness of the Duchess gratified him even more.

"He then made us sit down while he read us two new poems; both charming, and full of grace and naïveté; and one very affecting, being an address to the king, alluding to the death of his son. As he read, his wife stood by, and fearing we did not quite comprehend his language, she made a remark to that effect: to which he answered impatiently, 'Nonsense, —don't you see they are in tears.' This was unanswerable; and we were allowed to hear the poem to the end; and I certainly never listened to any thing more feelingly and energetically delivered.

"We had much conversation, for he was anxious to detain us, and, in the course of it, he told me that he had been by some accused of vanity. 'O,' he rejoined, 'what would you have! I am a child of nature, and cannot conceal my feelings; the only difference between me and a man of refinement is, that he knows how to conceal his vanity and exultation at success, which I let every body see.'" —*Béarn and the Pyrenees*, I. 369, *et seq.*

A Christmas Carol (p. 85)

The following description of Christmas in Burgundy is from M. Fertiault's *Coup d'oeil sur les Noels en Bourgogne*, prefixed to the Paris edition of *Les Noels Bourguignons de Bernard de la Monnoye'* *(Gui Barôzai)*, 1842.

"Every year, at the approach of Advent, people refresh their memories, clear their throats, and begin preluding, in the long evenings by the fireside, those carols whose invariable and eternal theme is the coming of the Messiah. They take from old closets pamphlets, little collections begrimed with dust and smoke, to which the press, and sometimes the pen, has consigned these songs; and as soon as the first Sunday of Advent sounds, they gossip, they gad about, they sit together by the fireside, sometimes at one house, sometimes at another, taking turns in paying for the chestnuts and white wine, but singing with one common voice the grotesque praises of the Little Jesus. There are very few villages even, which, during all the evenings of Advent, do not hear some of these curious canticles shouted in their streets, to the nasal drone of bagpipes. In this case the minstrel comes as a reinforcement to the singers at the fireside ; he brings and adds his dose of joy (spontaneous or mercenary, it matters little which) to the joy which breathes around the hearth-stone ; and when the voices vibrate and resound, one voice more is always welcome. There, it is not the purity of the notes which makes the concert, but the quantity, —*non qualitas, sed quantitas*; then, (to finish at once with the minstrel,) when the Saviour has at length been born in the manger, and the beautiful Christmas Eve is passed, the rustic piper makes his round among the houses, where every one compliments and thanks him, and, moreover, gives him in small coin the price of the shrill notes with which he has enlivened the evening entertainments.

"More or less, until Christmas Eve, all goes on in this way among our devout singers, with the difference of some gallons of wine or some hundreds of chestnuts. But this famous eve once come, the scale is pitched upon a higher key; the closing evening must be a memorable one. The toilet is begun at nightfall; then comes the hour of supper, admonishing divers appetites; and groups, as numerous as possible, are formed to take together this comfortable evening repast. The supper finished, a circle gathers around the hearth, which is arranged and set in order this evening after a particular fashion, and which at a later hour of the night is to become the object of special interest to the children. On the burning brands an enormous log has been placed. This log assuredly does not change its nature, but it changes its name during this evening: it is called the *Suche* (the Yule-log). 'Look you,' say they to the children, 'if you are good this evening, Noel' (for with children one must always personify) 'will rain down sugar-plums in the night.' And the children sit demurely, keeping as quiet as their turbulent little natures will permit. The groups of older persons, not always as orderly as the children, seize this good opportunity to surrender themselves with merry hearts and boisterous voices to the chanted worship of the miraculous Noel. For this final solemnitŷ, they have kept the most powerful, the most enthusiastic, the most electrifying carols. Noel! Noel! Noel! This magic word resounds on all sides; it seasons every sauce, it is served up with every course. Of the thousands of canticles which are heard on this famous eve, ninety-nine in a hundred begin and end with this word; which is, one may say, their Alpha and Omega, their crown and footstool. This last evening, the merry-making is prolonged. Instead of retiring at ten or eleven o'clock, as is generally done on all the preceding evenings, they wait for the stroke of midnight: this word sufficiently proclaims to what ceremony they are going to repair. For ten minutes or a quarter of an hour, the bells have been calling the faithful with a triple-bob-major; and each one, furnished with a little taper streaked with various colors, (the Christmas Candle,) goes through the crowded streets, where the lanterns are dancing like Will-o'-the-Wisps, at the impatient summons of the multitudinous chimes. It is the Midnight Mass. Once inside the church, they hear with more or less piety the Mass, emblematic of the coming of the Messiah. Then in tumult and great haste they return homeward, always in numerous groups; they salute the Yule-log; they pay homage to the hearth; they sit down at table; and, amid songs which reverberate louder than ever, make this meal of after-Christmas, so long looked for, so cherished, so joyous, so noisy, and which it has been thought fit to call, we hardly know why, *Rossignon*. The supper eaten at nightfall is no impediment, as you may imagine, to the appetite's returning; above all, if the going to and from church has made the devout eaters feel some little shafts of the sharp and biting north-wind. *Rossignon* then goes on merrily, —sometimes far into the morning hours; but, nevertheless, gradually throats grow hoarse, stomachs are filled, the Yule-log burns out, and at last the hour arrives when each one, as best he may, regains his domicile and his bed, and puts with himself between the sheets the material for a good sore-throat, or a good indigestion, for the morrow. Previous to this, care has been taken to place in the slippers, or wooden shoes, of the children, the sugar-plums, which shall be for them, on their waking, the welcome fruits of the Christmas log."

In the Glossary, the *Suche*, or Yule-log, is thus defined :

"This is a huge log, which is placed on the fire on Christmas Eve, and which in Burgundy is called, on this account, *lai Suche de Noei*. Then the father of the family, particularly among the middle classes, sings solemnly Christmas carols with his wife and children, the smallest of whom he sends into the corner to pray that the Yulelog may bear him some sugar-plums. Meanwhile, little parcels of them are placed under each end of the log, and the children come and pick them up, believing, in good faith, that the great log has borne them."

ABOUT THE AUTHOR

Henry Wadsworth Longfellow (1807-1882) was an American poet and educator. His best-known original works include "Paul Revere's Ride," "The Song of Hiawatha" and "Evangeline." He was the first American to completely translate Dante Alighieri's "Divine Comedy" and was one of the fireside poets from New England.

Longfellow wrote many lyric poems known for their musicality and often presenting stories of mythology and legend. He became the most popular American poet of his day and had success overseas. He has been criticized for imitating European styles and writing poetry that was too sentimental.

1807

—February 27, 1807: Birth of Henry Wadsworth Longfellow at Portland, Maine (which was at that time still part of Massachusetts). He was the son of Stephen Longfellow, a lawyer, and Zilch Wadsworth, daughter of Peleg Wadsworth, a general in the American Revolutionary War and a member of Congress. His mother was descended from Richard Warren, who was a passenger on the Mayflower. His Mayflower ancestors also included William Brewster and John and Priscilla Alden.

1810

—Longfellow att4ends a dame school at age three.
1812
—April 30: Louisiana becomes the 18th state to j
—June 18: The War of 1812 begins, during which the United States of America and its indigenous allies fought against the United Kingdom and its allies in British North America.

1813

—Longfellow is enrolled at age six at the private Portland Academy.
—A naval battle occurs between American and British sips offshore of New England. The treaty restored diplomatic relations and restored the pre-war borders of June 1812.

1814

—December 24: The Treaty of Ghent, a peace treaty concluding the War of 1812, was signed at Ghent, in the Netherlands, by representatives of the United States and the United Kingdom.

1816

—The statehood of Indiana is recognized, and Indiana becomes the 19th state of the Union. Indiana had previously been part of the Northwest Territory organized in 1787.

1817

—December 10: Mississippi becomes the 20th state admitted to the Union of the United States. Mississippi seceded from the Union and was restored to the Union in 1870, after the American Civil War.

1818

—Illinois achieved statehood after being part of the Northwest Territory for many years, becoming the 21st state of the Union.

1819

—December The statehood of Alabama is recognized. Alabama would later secede from the Union in 1861, rejoining the Union in 1868 after the American Civil War.

1820

—March 15: Maine becomes the 23rd state of the United States, as part of the Missouri Compromise, after residents voted to secede from the Commonwealth of Massachussets.

—Longfellow's first poem, "The Battle of Lovell's Pond," was published in the Portland Gazette on November 17, 1820. It was a patriotic and historical four-stanza poem.

—Nathaniel Hawthorne enrolls at Bowdoin College.

1821

—The former Missouri Territory is admitted to the Union as a slave state as part of the Missouri Compromise. Although the Confederacy recognized Missouri as its twelfth state, the secession was disputed and later regarded as not in effect.

1822

—Longfellow enrolls at Bowdoin College in Brunswick, Maine, along with his brother Stephen. His grandfather was a founder of the college and his father was a trustee. Here he met Nathaniel Hawthorne, a lifelong friend.

1824

—Nearly 40 minor poems by Longfellow are published between January 1824 and his graduation in 1825, many of these at the short-lived Boston periodical, The United States Literary Gazette."

1825

—Longfellow graduates from Bowdoin College, fourth in his class

and elected to Phi Beta Kappa. He gave the student commence-
ment address.
—Longfellow is offered a job as professor of modern languages at
his alma mater, on condition that he prepare by touring Europe
and learning Romance languages.

1826

—January 30: Washington Irving, while living in Paris, is invited
to travel to Madrid to inspect the Spanish archives in the library
of the American consul.
—In May, Longfellow travels from New York to Le Havre, in
France, aboard the ship 'Cadmus.' He spent three years in Europe,
visiting France, Spain, Italy, Germany, and England. During his
time abroad he learned French, Italian, Spanish, Portuguese, and
German, mostly without formal instruction. While in Madrid, he
met with Washington Irving, who encouraged his writing.
—July 4: Former U.S. Presidents Thomas Jefferson and John Adams
both die on the 50th anniversary of the signing of the United States
Declaration of Independence.

1827

—In the United Kingdom, George Canning succeeds Lord Liver-
pool as British prime minister.
—The term "socialist" is coined by Robert Owen in his London
periodical, The Co-operative Magazine and Monthly Herald.

1828

—January: Washington Irving's book, "A History of the Life and
Voyages of Christopher Columbus," was published.
—The first substantial praise of Longfellow's work is published,
by John Neal, a fellow native of Portland, Maine, in the January
23, 1828 issue of his magazine, "The Yankee." He wrote: "As for
Mr. Longfellow, he has a fine genius and a pure and safe taste,…"
—December 3: Andrew Jackson is elected President of the United
States, defeating incumbent John Quincy Adams.

1829

—March 22; Greece receives autonomy from the Ottoman Empire.
—July 23: In the United States, William Burt obtains the first patent for a form of typewriter, the typographer.
—In mid-August, Longfellow returns to the United States.
—August 27: Longfellow wrote to the president of Bowdoin that he was turning down the professorship because he considered the $600 salary "disproportionate to the duties required." The trustees raised his salary to $800 with an additional $100 to serve as the college's librarian, which required one hour of work per day. While teaching at the college he translated textbooks from French, Italian, and Spanish.

1831

—July 21: Leopold of Saxe-Coburg-Gotha is inaugurated as the first King of the Belgians in Brussels.
—September 14, Longfellow marries Mary Storer, a childhood friend from Portland, Maine.

1832

—February 28: Charles Darwin and the crew of HMS Beagle arrive at South America for the first time.
—Greece is recognized as a sovereign nation by the Treaty of Constantinople, ending the Greek War of Independence.

1833

—Washington Irving's book, "Tales of the Alhambra," a book of short stories, is published.
—Longfellow's first published book was a translation of poetry by the medieval Spanish poet, Jorge Manrique, "Coplas de Don Jorge Manrique."
—Publication of several nonfiction and fiction prose pieces inspired by Irving, including "The Indian Summer" and "The Bald Eagle."

1834

—Longfellow receives a letter from Harvard College offering him the Smith Professorship of Modern Languages, with the stipulation that he spend a year abroad. He and his wife travel to Europe, where he studies German as well as Dutch, Danish, Swedish, Finnish, and Icelandic.

—The Spanish Inquisition, which had begun in the 15th century, is suppressed by royal decree.

1835

—Publication of "Outer-Mer: A Pilgrimage Beyond the Sea," a collection of Prose works by Longfellow. The term "outer-mer" is French for "overseas."

—September 7: Charles Darwin arrives at the Galapagos Islands, aboard HMS Beagle.

—November 29: Death of Longfellow's first wife, after a miscarriage. Her body was shipped home to the United States for burial at Mount Auburn Cemetery near Boston.

—December 28: The Second Seminole War led by Osceola breaks out.

1836

—Longfellow returns to the United States and assumes the professorship at Harvard.

—June 15: Arkansas is the 25th state admitted into the United States of America. Arkansas seceded from the Union in 1861 and rejoined in 186, after the American Civil War.

—Sam Houston is elected as the first president of the Republic of Texas.

1837

—January 26: Michigan becomes the 26th state of the United States, following the Toledo War, a boundary dispute with Ohio, in which Ohio was granted the Toledo region and Michigan was given the western part of the Upper Peninsula.

—During the spring Longfellow has rented rooms at the Craigie House, built in 1759, which served as the headquarters of George Washington during the Siege of Boston. Previous boarders included Jared Sparks, Edward Everett, and Joseph Emerson Worcester. The house is preserved as the Longfellow House-Washington's Headquarters National Historic Site.

—Charles Dickens's "Oliver Twist" begins publication in serial form in London.

1838

—Longfellow writes the poem, "Footsteps of Angels," said to be about his late wife.

—June 28: The coronation of Queen Victoria takes place at Westminster Abbey in London.

—July 4: The Iowa Territory is formally established after a bill signed by U.S President Martin Van Buren on June 12.

1839

—Publication of Longfellow's first poetry collection, "Voices of the Night," his first book of poetry. Although most of the book was translations, it included nine original poems and seven poems that he had written as a teenager.

—During Longfellow's seven-year long courtship of Frances "Fanny" Appleton, whose family lived at Beacon Hill in Boston. He often walked from Cambridge to the Appleton home by crossing the Boston Bridge. That bridge was replaced in 1906 with a new bridge later renamed as the Longfellow Bridge.

—Publication of "Hyperion: A Romance," a romance novel, whose main character, Paul Flemming, travels through Germany and falls in love with an Englishwoman who rejects him. The semi-autobiographical novel hints of his own travels, his atheistic beliefs and his own as yet unsuccessful courtship. The novel's descriptions of Germany would later inspire its use as a companion travel guide for American tourists in that country.

1840?

—Longfellow takes a six-month leave of absence from Harvard to attend a health spa in the former Marienberg Benedictine Convent at Boppard in Germany

1841

—Publication of Longfellow's "Ballads and Other Poems," which included "The Village Blacksmith" and "The Wreck of the Hesperus."
—January 26: Britain occupies Hong Kong, an island with a population of 7,500.
—March 4: William Henry Harrison is sworn in as the ninth President of the United States.
—April 6: John Tyler is sworn in as the tenth President of the United States, two days after Harrison's death of pneumonia.

1842

—Publication of the drama "The Spanish Student: A Paly in Three Acts," a play in which he reflects on his time in Spain in the 1820s.
—Publication of Longfellow's "Poems on Slavery," his first public support of abolitionism and anti-slavery efforts. Most of the poems were written at sea in October 1842. The poems were later reprinted as anti-slavery tracts in 1843, and included: "To William E. Channing," "The Slave's Dream," "The Good Part," "The Slave in the Dismal Swamp," "The Slave Singing at Midnight," "The Witnesses," "The Quadroon Girl," and "The Warning."

1843

—Longfellow marries Frances Elizabeth Appleton.
—Nathan Appleton, the father of Longfellow's wife, purchases the former Craigie house as a wedding present, and Longfellow lives there for the rest of his life.

1844

—Birth of Charles Appleton Longfellow
—Publication of "Poets and Poetry of Europe," with translations by Longfellow.

1845

—March 3: Florida is admitted to the Union as the 27th state. Florida, an area previously contested by Spain and Great Britain, had been ceded to the United States in 1819. Florida seceded from the Union in 1861 and rejoined in 1868, after the American Civil War.
—March 4: James K. Polk (1795-1849) is sworn in as the 11th president of the United States of America.
—Birth of Ernest Wadsworth Longfellow
—Publication of "The Belfry of Bruges and Other Poems," a poetry collection.
—Publication of "The Waif: A Collection of Poems," an anthology of poems by various authors, to which Longfellow contributed "Proem."
—December 29: Texas is recognized as the 28th state of the United States.

1846

—December 28, 1846: Iowa becomes the 29th state in the Union.

1847

—April 7: Birth of Fanny Longfellow, the Longfellows' first daughter. During childbirth, Dr. Nathan Cooley Keep administered ether to the mother as the first obstetric anestthetic in the United States.
—November 1: Publication of Longfellow's epic poem, "Evangeline: A Tale of Acadia."

1848

—May 29: Wisconsin becomes the 30th state to join the United States.

1849

—Publication of "Kavanagh: A Tale," a story of a country romance, in which Mr. Churchill, a school teacher, who has always planned to write a romance, but whose procrastination has never allowed him to start, until late in life he resigns himself to his "destiny."
—March 4: Major General Zachary Taylor (1784-1850) is sworn in as the 12th president of the United States of America.

1850

—Birth of Alice Mary Longfellow
—Publication of "The Seaside and the Fireside," a poetry collection.
—March 4: Millard Fillmore (1800-1874) is sworn in as the 13th president of the United States.

1851

—Publication of "The Golden Legend," a poem.

1852

—Publication of "The Poetical Works of Henry Wadsworth Long-fellow," a poetry collection, in London, with illustrations by John Gilbert.

1853

—Birth of Edith Longfellow
—March 4: Franklin Pierce (1804-1869) is sworn in as the 14th president of the United States of America.
—June 13: Longfellow hosts a farewell dinner party at his Cambridge home for his friend Nathaniel Hawthorne., who was preparing to move overseas.

1854

—Longfellow retired from his teaching position at Harvard to focus on his writing

1855

—Birth of Anne Allegra Longfellow
—Publication of "The Song of Hiawatha," an epic poem in trochaic tetrameter, featuering Native American characters. The epic tells the fictional adventures of an Ojibwe warrior named Hiawatha and the tragedy of his love for Minnehaha, a Dakota woman.

1857

—March 4: James Buchanan (1791-1868) is sworn in as the 15th president of the United States of America.

1858

—May 11: The Minnesota Territory is admitted to the Union as the 32nd state in the United States.
—Publicaiton of "The Courtship of Miles Standish and Other Poems," a poetry collection. "The Coursthip of Miles Standish" is a narrative poem, written in dactylic hexameter, about the early days of Plymouth Colony, the colonial settlement established in America by the Mayfflower pilgrims. The poem was among the most enduringly popular of Longfellow's works.

1859

—February 14: Oregon is admitted to the Union as the 33rd state of the United States.
—Longfellow is awarded an honorary doctorate of laws from Harvard.

1860

—April 6: Longfellow writes the poem, "Paul Revere's Ride," commemorating the actions of Paul Revere on April 18, 1775, when he was said to warn American patriot defenders of the approaching British, although not a historically accurate account. It was written the day after Longfellow visited the Old North Church in Boston and climbed its tower It was first published in the January 1861 issue of 'The Atlantic Monthly.' Longfellow's family was said to have a connection to the historical Paul Revere in that his maternal grandfather, Peleg Wadsworth, had been Revere's commander during the Penobscot Expedition.

1861

—January 29: Kansas becomes the 39th state to join the United States.
—March 4: Abraham Lincoln (1809-1865) is sworn in as the 16th president of the United States of America.
—April 12: Start of the American Civil War, in which the Union states and the states of the southern Confederacy fought over issues of slavery.
—July 9: Longfellow's wife was sealing an envelope with hot sealing wax, or lighting a match, when her dress caught fire and her body was badly burned.
—July 10: Death of Francis Appleton, Longfellow's wife.
—Death of Longfellow's second wife, after sustaining burns when her dress caught fire. The distraught Longfellow was himself was injured by burns on his face, after trying to quench the flames with his body, and after that wore a beard to conceal the scars.

1863

—January 1: The Emancipation Proclamation was a presidential proclamation and executive order issued by Abraham Lincoln granted freedom to the slaves of the Confederacy.
—June 20: West Virginia is admitted to the Union as the 35th state of the United States, after seceding from the Confederate State of Virginia.
—July 1-3: The Battle of Gettysburg, fought near the town of Gettysburg in Pennsylvania, in which Union forces halted the Confederates' invasion to the north, was considered a turning point of the American Civil War.
—Publication of "The Legend of Rabbi Ben Levi," a poem telling about Yehoshua ben Levi, a Jewish rabbi and scholar of the Talmud

who lived in the land of Israel in the first half of the third century, and taught in the city of Lod, and was known for his debates of theological matters.

—November 23: Publication of "Tales of a Wayside Inn," a poetry collection, in whcih a group of people gathered at the Wayside Inn in Sudbury, Massachusetts, (about 20 miles from the poet's home in Cambridge), each take turns each telling a story in a variety of poetic forms and styles. The characters are said to be loosely based on actual persons of Longfellow's acquaintance. Includes his previously published poem, "Paul Revere's Ride," and "The Saga of King Olaf." Includes the "second flight" of "Bords of Passage").

—December 25: Longfellow writes the poem "Christmas Bells," which becomes the lyrics of the beloved Christmas carol, "I Heard the Bells on Christmas Day."

1864

—Longfellow launches the "Dante Club," of friends who meet weekly to help with perfecting the translation of Dante Alighieri's "Divine Comedy." Guests included regulars William Dean Howells, James Russell Lowell, and Charles Eliot Norton.

—October 31: Nevada becomes the 36th state of the Union.

1865

—Longfellow's poem, "Christmas Bells," is published in "Our Young Folks," a juvenile magazine published by Ticknor and Fields.

—Publication of "Household Poems," a poetry collection.

—April 9: Confederate General Robert E. Lee surrenders to Union General Ulysses S. Grant after the Battle of Appomattox Court House.

—April 15: Andrew Johnson (1808-1875) is sworn in as the 17th president of the United States of America, following the assassination of Abraham Lincoln.

1867

—March 1: Nebraska becomes the 37th state of the Union.

—Publication of "The Divine Comedy," Longfellows translation of

Dante Alighieri's work, in three volumes, although revisions continued and the work went through four printings in the first year.
—Publication of "Flower-de-Luce," a poetry collection.

1868

—Publication of "The New England Tragedies," containing two dramatic plays in verse reflecting on events in the early days of New England. The play "John Endicott" dramatizes the clash between the Puritans and the Quakers and the play "Giles Corey of the Salem Farms" is about the Salem witchcraft trials.

1869

—March 4: General Ulysses S. Grant (1822-1885) is sworn in as the 18th president of the United States of America.

1871

—Publication of Longfellow's translation of Dante Alighieri's "The Divine Tragedy," in three volumes.

1872

—Publication of "Christus: A Mystery," a trilogy composed of three previous works: "The Golden Legend," The New England Tragedies," and "The Divine Tragedy."
—Publication of "Three Books of Song," a poetry collection (including the second part of "Tales of a Wayside Inn").
—Longfellow's poem, "Christmas Bells," is set to music by the English organist, John Baptiste Calkin, using a melody called "Waltham." Other melodies have been used, including the 1845 melody of "Mainzer" and a 1956 tune by Johnny Marks, which was popularized by a Bing Crosby recording.

1873

—Publication of "Aftermath," (comprising the third part of "Tales of a Wayside Inn," and the "third flight" of "Birds of Passage").

1874

—Samuel Ward helped Longfellow with the selling of a poem, "The Hanging of the Crane," to the 'New York Ledger' for $3,000, the highest price ever paid for a poem.
—Longfellow oversees the publication of a 31-volume anthology, called "Poems of Places," which collected poems representing geographical locations, including European, Asian, and Arabian countries.

1875

—Publication of "The Masque of Pandora and Other Poems," a poetry collection.

1876

—August 1: Colorado is admitted to the Union, after being organized as the Territory of Colorado since 1861.

1877

—March 4: Rutherford B. Hayes (1822-1893) is sworn in as the 19th president of the United States of America.

1878

—Publication of "Kêramos and Other Poems," a poetry collection.

1880

—Publication of "Ultima Thule," a poetry collection.

1881

—March 4: James A. Garfield ((1831-1881) is sworn in as the 20th president of the United States of America.

1882

—March 24: Death of Longfellow at his home in Cambridge, surrounded by family. He is buried at Mount Auburn Cemetery in Cambridge, Massachusetts.
—Publication of "In the Harbor," a poetry collection.

—Publication of "Michael Angelo: A Frament," (incomplete, published posthumously).